RHODODENDRONS AND AZALEAS

There is a rhododendron for almost every garden and every situation. Among the great number of species and hybrids in this immense family, there are many dwarfs, suitable even for the rock garden, many others of intermediate height, and yet others which eventually reach tree-like proportions and heights of fifty feet or more. There is a very wide range of colours available in both species and hybrids, while the plants are even more variable in size and form of flower and leaf than they are in height.

Frederick Street, who is well known for his exhibits of hardy hybrid rhododendrons and for his writings on the family, describes the characteristics of each type and gives detailed lists of recommended varieties. He also deals fully with the many aspects of cultivation.

An Amateur Gardening Handbook

AMATEUR GARDENING HANDBOOK NO 19

RHODODENDRONS AND AZALEAS

FREDERICK STREET
(author of *Hardy Rhododendrons*)

19

W. H. & L. COLLINGRIDGE LTD

2-10 TAVISTOCK STREET COVENT GARDEN LONDON WC2

FIRST PUBLISHED IN 1957

The Amateur Gardening Handbooks
are published by
W. H. & L. Collingridge Limited
2-10 Tavistock Street, London, WC2
and printed and bound in England by
Hazell Watson & Viney Limited
Aylesbury, Bucks
© *W. H. & L. Collingridge Ltd. 1957*

SECOND IMPRESSION 1966

CONTENTS

5

ILLUSTRATIONS

BY JOAN MILROY

ACKNOWLEDGEMENTS

I SHOULD like to express my thanks to Lord Crawley, who helped me with suggestions for the list of species, and to the Editor of the Royal Horticultural Society's publications for permission to quote from *The Rhododendron Handbook*.

FREDERICK STREET

Heathermead Nursery,
West End,
Nr. Woking.

INTRODUCTION

THERE can be no doubt that the rhododendron is the finest evergreen flowering shrub that may be grown out of doors in the British Isles. It is a plant that has risen steadily in popularity—and it is still rising but now more swiftly. It is no longer a plant that is considered to be a delicate exotic for the enjoyment of a few people who own gardens in the softer parts of the country. It is the evergreen for everyman: it even seems to be competing with the aucuba to decorate London's buildings and streets. There is only one essential condition for good cultivation —the soil must be acid, that is to say, without lime either natural or artificial.

This is a practical book for the practical gardener. It is not for the botanist or the expert. It is intended for the man who can grow rhododendrons, but does not yet do so and wishes to try. On the other hand, it may well be useful to one who already does grow one or two plants and wishes to grow more and know a little more about them.

Anyone can grow rhododendrons on an acid soil, but not necessarily all rhododendrons. For there are some varieties and species that are more suited to some places than others. Years ago—towards the end of the seventeenth century and the beginning of the eighteenth century —the rhododendron was grown chiefly in the Mile End Road. And it would still be possible to grow certain varieties in that part of London, where the smoke and the grime and the smog are at their worst. These are probably the worst possible conditions that could be found. Between those and the best—the milder parts of the country where the soft air of the Gulf Stream caresses the leaves with hidden moisture—there is a vast range of different conditions, and there is a vast range of different rhododendrons to suit them all.

And now we come to a paradox that puzzles many. I have said that the rhododendron is the finest flowering evergreen for the British Isles—and so it is. But there are, or were, a few deciduous rhododendrons. Nowadays there are many—for the azalea is exactly the same as the rhododendron to all botanical intents and purposes.

The botanist found that rhododendrons and azaleas were the same; therefore they are now all classified as one plant. Yet botanists' definitions are not always the best for the practical gardener. Many plants often need separate classification. Accordingly the first part of this book divides the rhododendron (and the azalea) into different types that are not necessarily rigid. I have put them into gardening categories for general use, showing the position and climate and situation that are best for each. The following is my arrangement, showing the reason for the different groups.

Hardy Hybrid Rhododendrons   These are the varieties that are probably the best known. They are, in fact, what is usually understood by 'a rhododendron'. Many plants have their personalities, their stars—the geranium has Paul Crampel, the clematis has *jackmanii*, the apple has Cox's Orange Pippin and the rhododendron has 'Pink Pearl'. And the qualities of 'Pink Pearl' are the qualities of the hardy hybrid rhododendron—strong growing, hardy under all conditions, large flowering, good colour, free flowering and, above all, reliability—the quality of giving a good display each year, even under the most trying conditions. You will find this type of rhododendron growing throughout the length and breadth of the country, from the exhaust-laden hot air of Parliament Square to the wilds of Scotland.

Dwarf Evergreen Rhododendrons Although these may not be so universally popular as the hardy hybrid rhododendron, I include them next because they may be grown

1. *Dwarf evergreen rhododendron flower.*

in many parts of the country in pots or pans or tubs. They come well within the range of the alpine house and the rock garden, and they are small enough to allow special soil to be provided in gardens where lime lurks ready to inhibit the roots. But the dwarf evergreen rhododendrons are not the same easy-going plants as the hardy hybrids. They do need a little more care and attention—particularly in the way of water. But their neat compact habit and their individuality make them better known and probably of wider use than some of the taller, and equally beautiful, species.

Deciduous Azalea Almost equal to the hardy hybrid rhododendron in being generally well known are the deciduous azaleas. Most people will say when you mention an azalea that they admire those that are 'flame'-coloured—a shade that is well known to the fairer sex in matters of fashion but not, I fear, recognized by the horticultural colour chart! It is, I understand, a delicate apricot shot with orange and pink (it is the predominant colour of the 'mollis' group). And a very beautiful shade it is, too. However, there are equally good assets in all the azaleas, not the least being scent beyond compare and autumn foliage almost as lovely as the flowers. There are many other types and many other colours from white and soft yellow to the most brilliant orange-scarlet.

Dwarf Evergreen Azaleas For colour in the garden these, in my opinion, are more lovely than the dwarf rhododendrons. They have a wider range of colour, they are easier to grow, and they take fourth place only because they balance the deciduous azaleas, as the dwarf evergreen rhododendrons balance the hardy hybrids, purely from the point of view of classification. They all mix freely in the garden, with certain reservations.

Dwarf Evergreen Indoor Azaleas These are the varieties that can be seen in the florists' shops at Christmas-time.

11

To many people they are the best known. They are essentially greenhouse plants and are not suitable for the garden. They are expensive, they are tender and they require special treatment. And because they are generally well

2. *The flower of an indoor evergreen azalea.*

known, many people think that all azaleas are the same. Nothing could be more untrue.

Rhododendron Species A species, as opposed to a hybrid, is a plant of definite botanical form that is found growing naturally in the wild and which will reproduce itself from seed without variation. The ancestry of the hardy hybrids is very mixed, and seedlings from these will be more so.

Under this section I hope to describe some of those that are suitable for the garden. This chapter takes the form of a short guide to the Royal Horticultural Society's Rhododendron Show held early in May (usually three weeks before the Chelsea Show) each year.

Rhododendrons for the Warm Garden or the Greenhouse
This group includes some of the most beautiful plants of

the whole range. But they are some of the most difficult. They require ideal conditions and sometimes more. However, it would be wrong in a book that is intended to cover

3. *A rhododendron for the cool greenhouse.*

all types to leave them out. Accordingly, I will describe the best and their fads and fancies.

First Crosses and 'Blue-blooded' Rhododendrons These are the varieties for the coming expert. They are hybrids between two species or between first hybrids of those species. *The Rhododendron Handbook* of the Royal Horticultural Society gives their breeding, and the creation of a new rhododendron of merit is probably the culmination of the rhododendron grower's career.

13

In order to avoid unnecessary repetition, I have listed a brief selection of all the various types under their various headings. There are many more of each sort besides those

4. *An example of a 'first cross' between two species.*

that I have named and the selection is, I hope, as unbiased as it is possible for one man to make.

The second half of the book deals with the cultivation of the plants. There are many similarities between all the different sections, but where special treatment is required I have given it special mention.

CHAPTER ONE

HARDY HYBRID RHODODENDRONS

THIS group of rhododendrons is the best known and, in my opinion, the hardy hybrids are responsible for the present popularity of the rhododendron in this country. Most of them may be grown easily in any place where the soil is acid. Strong evergreen flowering shrubs, they vary

5. *Bud and truss of a hardy hybrid rhodo-dendron.*

in habit from compact bushes 3 ft. high to large shrubs over 10 ft. in height. The flowers are held in trusses. The different varieties flower from January to June.

Parentage They have been raised principally from seven species—*R. ponticum* from Spain, Portugal and Asia Minor, *R. caucasicum* from a little farther north in the Caucasus Mountains, *R. maximum* and *R. catawbiense* from the United States and *R. arboreum, R. cam-*

panulatum and *R. griffithianum* from the Himalayas. All these, except *R. griffithianum*, were used to raise the first hybrid rhododendrons. Probably the most important of the species in the first hybrids were *catawbiense* and *arboreum*. From *catawbiense* the hardy hybrid has gained that part of its name that it so rightly deserves—hardy. *Rhododendron arboreum* gave the colour to the first hybrids—it has many different forms and the best are a bright red. It is said that *Rhododendron* John Waterer, a variety still grown today, is a direct cross between these two. While it may not necessarily be up to the standard for all gardens nowadays, it is still valuable because of the hardiness that it inherits from *catawbiense*. For this reason *catawbiense* is probably one of the most important rhododendrons that has ever been introduced into this country. It may not have the exciting colour of some of the species from the Himalayas, but it has given us tough plants of good habit. The flowers of *catawbiense* are mauve and somewhat similar to those of *ponticum* but the habit is compact and bushy. On its own, or when it is planted near to some of the later-flowering white varieties, it is still a plant that commands attention.

The qualities given by the other species that played a part in the raising of the early varieties are these—*ponticum* gives vigorous growth, *caucasicum* gives early flowers and bushy habit, *maximum* gives attractive foliage and a later flower, *campanulatum* gives hardiness and another form of leaf. All these were used and many varieties were raised. These were then again crossed with one another to produce further hybrids that were improvements on the first generation. Many of these are still grown and are justly popular. But they are not the best, except for one or two brilliant exceptions, that are available today.

Rhododendron griffithianum In 1849 *Rhododendron griffithianum* was introduced into this country from the Himalayas. Although it is tender it has played a great part in the development of the hardy hybrid by giving added quality that could not have been found among the early parents. The flower of the original plant is large and waxy, often as much as 5 or 6 in. in diameter. The truss is large, loose and gracefully formed. The famous *Rhododendron* Pink Pearl owes much of its beauty to this species.

This wonderful plant was crossed with the second group of hybrids and the resulting plants were crossed again. This gave many fine varieties which were selected to be hardy and to have this touch of glamour which had come to England from India. The best that have been raised in recent years are those that possess, in nice balance, the finest qualities of these seven species.

Other species One or two other species have made their mark. *R. thomsonii*, also from India, has given another shade of red and a slightly different shape of flower, *R. campylocarpum*, again from India, has given some yellow-flowered varieties, while *R. fortunei* from China has brought a richer texture to the petals of some rhododendrons.

The Uses of Hardy Hybrids Today there are all sorts of hardy hybrids—tall and thin, short and fat, early flowering, late flowering, and in all colours from dead white to

17

deep red. Because of this they have many uses. They may be planted as single plants to form specimen bushes or trees. They are suitable for growing in pots and tubs. They may be used in a mixed shrub border or even in the herbaceous border. They can be planted as a hedge, or in groups, or as a complete border on their own. A few shrubs mix well with the hardy rhododendrons. Japanese maples, birches, hardy heathers, pernettyas, pieris and vacciniums seem to be their natural friends. But the hardy hybrid rhododendron remains the most satisfactory plant to grow and, when it is in bloom, the most exciting plant to see.

In Chapter Nine I have made the selection of those that I think are best, taking the balance of hardiness, colour, size of flower and truss, texture of petal, habit of growth and foliage.

CHAPTER TWO

DWARF RHODODENDRONS

ALTHOUGH the dwarf rhododendrons are not every-body's plant, I have put them next on the list because they could be. Furthermore, there is one that is the easiest of all rhododendrons to grow because it is not particular about the soil in which it grows—it will even grow in one that contains lime.

The dwarf rhododendrons are compact shrubs, from creeping plants of a few inches to modest bushes of 3 ft. Many have attractive foliage, often aromatic; the pre-dominant flower colour is mauve—from lilac-pink to reddish purple. The flowers are small but plentiful, and in many different shapes from saucers to pincushions (with pins). They may be planted in a number of posi-tions; the rock garden, the heather garden and the front of shrub borders (particularly plantings of rhododendrons and azaleas) being the most obvious.

The Alpine Rose But I intend to describe the Alpine Rose (*R. hirsutum*) in detail for two reasons: because it is the oldest rhododendron in cultivation in Great Britain, and because it may be grown in any type of soil, includ-ing lime. It is a neat evergreen shrub growing to a height of from 2 to 3 ft., with a mass of small flowers in June. The colour can be anything from deep pink to near red. Its close relation is *R. ferrugineum*, which is also known as the Alpine Rose, and the two are often mixed up. *R.*

ferrugineum blooms in July and August in the Alps. These are two of the few rhododendrons that are wild in Europe and they are probably the best known.

Other European Species *R. chrysanthum*, a somewhat rare and difficult plant, comes from Siberia, and *R. lapponicum*—also not very easy to grow—comes from Lapland. But *R. lapponicum* has given its name to a series of rhododendrons that all have the same family likeness although many of the best come from China. They are nearly all in shades of blue and purple.

Blue Hybrids A number of hybrids with the blue members of the *lapponicum* series have been made with some of the best blue forms of *Rhododendron augustinii*—a tall species from China. The advantages of these (the best being Blue Tit and Blue Diamond) are that they are better in colour than the dwarfs, and larger flowered, but they are much more hardy than *R. augustinii*. The habit is in between, with an ultimate size of 3 ft. × 4 ft.

Rhododendron saluenense Another plant that has given its name to a series of dwarfs is *R. saluenense*. Many of these species have been collected at great heights—14,000 ft. above sea-level—and consequently they are used to frost. But frost is not everything, and the atmosphere of Upper Tibet is not quite the same as that of Upper Tooting. Neither is the soil. Up among the Lamas the soil is thin and poor, the atmosphere is rarefied and damp. So it follows that if the dwarf rhododendrons are given a comparatively rich soil with more moisture below than above they are apt to grow out of character. They will be taller and even a bit rank. Because of this they are better in the wetter parts of the country, particularly those that belong to the *saluenense* series.

Other Hybrids The dwarf rhododendrons are not all difficult to grow—some are very easy and I have indicated these in the list in Chapter Nine. One or two hybrids are easier still—mostly the blues I have mentioned—while *R. forrestii* (formerly *R. repens*), a temperamental creeping scarlet species, has given some hybrids that are simple to grow compared with its own fads and fancies. One of these fads is a lack of reliability in flowering—it cannot be relied on to give a good show every year. Sometimes it passes this unfortunate trait on to its hybrids and sometimes not. I mention this because there are a number of new dwarf hybrids from *R. forrestii* that have been raised in Germany and which will be coming on the market in the course of the next few years. I cannot say very much about them as they have not yet been tried out in this country. Those that inherit the habits of growth of *forrestii* plus the size of flower and reliability of the hardy hybrids with which they have been crossed should be very good indeed. Similar crosses have been made with *R. williamsianum*—a dwarf pink with cup-shaped flowers and heart-shaped leaves, but just a shade tender.

Cultivation Apart from the Alpine Rose, which will suffer a lime soil, the dwarf rhododendrons can be catered for with pockets of peat in gardens where normally no acid soil exists. They are ideal for pot culture and offer a rich reward to the enthusiastic alpine grower. (Full details of cultivation are in Chapters Eleven and Twelve.)

Colour Schemes Although most of the dwarf rhododendrons are blue, mauve and purple, this does not mean that they are of little value. They can be beautiful on their own and magnificent with yellow. The earlier-flowering varieties of *Azalea mollis* (Hortulanus Witte and Golden Sunlight, for example) can be very fine with some of the blue dwarfs, both species and hybrids. And as a suggestion for something that is a poem of colour, *R. russatum* planted behind the ordinary primrose will be lyrical in the harmony of rich purple and soft yellow. And this being one of the loveliest colour schemes that come in rhododendrons, another use for the dwarf blues and purples is to plant them in front of the hardy hybrid yellows, using the shorter hardy hybrids and the taller dwarfs.

CHAPTER THREE

DECIDUOUS AZALEAS

STRICTLY speaking, there is no such plant as an azalea. The azaleas are part of the great family of rhododendron and they make up one of the 'series' in that family (rhododendron species being divided into series according to their botanical characteristics). They have become generally known as azaleas, although individually they are rhododendrons—and that is how I hope to call them throughout the rest of this book.

This chapter deals with the deciduous varieties, those that lose their leaves in the winter.

They are medium to tall shrubs with flowers a little smaller than rhododendrons, often beautifully scented and often with colour of staggering brilliance. They may be planted in groups, as single specimens, in shrub borders, in herbaceous borders—almost anywhere. Shade from the hottest sun will help to make the flowers last longer. But too much shade will cancel out the autumn colour of the foliage. Three o'clock is the ideal time for the shadow to start.

The Species   The deciduous azaleas are probably older, so far as cultivation in this country is concerned, than the hardy rhododendrons. The first came over in 1680 from Virginia, sent by a missionary, John Bannister, to Bishop Compton, who was then Bishop of London. This variety was 'The Swamp Honeysuckle', *Rhododendron* *viscosum.* Some sixty years later another variety was introduced, the 'Pinkster Bloom', *R. nudiflorum,* also from North America. Then, in 1793, an outstanding variety came from the Crimea to Belgium and England *via* the Imperial Botanic Gardens, St Petersburg—this was *R. luteum,* better known as *Azalea pontica,* with its yellow flowers and delicious scent. In the early nineteenth century an important species, *R. molle,* was introduced from Japan and China. There are two species that seem to be very closely related—*R. molle,* and *R. japonica,* so closely related as to be almost the same plant. Several other species have been introduced, mostly from North America, and they have all played their parts. One of the most important was probably *R. occidentalis,* which came to us from California—a late-flowering species with large flowers that are well scented.

Many hybrids were produced, probably more mixed in their ancestry than the hardy hybrid rhododendrons. Each species has been used and various hybrids have been crossed and recrossed one with the other so that it is now hard to define one azalea as being of one particular type. Several of the older hybrids can be classified in two or even three of the various groups.

The Ghent Azaleas The oldest of these groups is the 'Ghent' azaleas—raised in Ghent between 1805 and 1830. The hybridization was done by a baker who was interested in plants; they were not the result of work by a professional gardener or nurseryman. They combine the good qualities of several species—the original *R. viscosum* with its late-flowering period and strong scent, the

24

strength and vigour of *R. luteum* with its yellow flowers and, again, strong scent, but probably the most important of all was the vivid colour that came from *R. calendulaceum*, discovered by a Frenchman, André Michaux, in

6. *An old-type Ghent azalea.*

North Carolina and sent to France and Belgium in 1806. The baker, a Monsieur P. Mortier, sold the parent plants of his new race of hybrids to a nurseryman, Monsieur Verschaffelt, in 1830, who again carried on the work of hybridization. He and other Belgian nurserymen produced more varieties, some of which have double flowers.

The Ghent azaleas are late flowering, tall growing, very hardy and many of them have a beautiful perfume. If they have a fault, it is that the foliage of some of them appears at the same time as the flowers, which are not quite so well displayed as a result.

The Mollis Azaleas Historically, the next groups to be raised were those that are now known as '*mollis*' or '*mollis* × *sinensis*' or '*molle-japonicum*' azaleas. These are hybrids between the three types of the azalea that is most commonly known as *Azalea mollis*. Many beautiful hybrids have been raised and there are none that could be called bad. Their characteristics are that the flowers appear before the foliage, and are thus better displayed than those of the Ghent azaleas. However, they flower earlier in the year, so that they are inclined to be cut by spring frosts. Their normal flowering period is during the early part of May, while the Ghents do not flower before the end of May or even in June. The mollis azalea hybrids are perfectly hardy and will withstand the most trying conditions. Most of the work in raising these hybrids was done in Holland; very little was done in this country.

Occidentalis Hybrids The next important phase was the introduction of *Azalea occidentalis* from California to England and thence to Boskoop in Holland. Here the firm of M. Koster and Sons raised some fine hybrids, which are still widely grown today. These had the advantage of the mollis azaleas in that the flowers were large and formed into trusses, they were also late flowering and well scented.

Knap Hill Azaleas Different varieties of all these hybrids

26

found their way to England about the middle of the nineteenth century. They were again hybridized and much of
the work was done by the late Anthony Waterer of the
Knap Hill Nursery. He produced a race of azaleas that
combined all the best qualities of all the different groups.
These have become known as the Knap Hill azaleas and
there are various developments from these. Probably the
best are the Exbury strain, which have brilliant colours,
large flowers, many with prominent stamens, most of
them are well scented and they also have good autumn
colour.

Selection I have arranged the lists in Chapter Nine to
show the best of all the deciduous azaleas.

Very often some of the finest colours are obtainable as
seedlings raised from these various types, particularly the
mollis azaleas and the Exbury strain. These are less expensive than the named varieties but equally vigorous, if
not a little more so. For general effect they are probably
quite as good as the named sorts and they show a con-
siderable saving.

CHAPTER FOUR

DWARF EVERGREEN HARDY AZALEAS

THESE are often known as 'Japanese' azaleas because most of them come from that country. And they are Japanese in habit, for we connect that description with a particular form of shrub—one that seems to grow in layers, spreading outwards, fanwise. They are mostly dwarf shrubs, with small evergreen leaves, varying in height from 1 ft. to, sometimes, 4 ft. when fully grown.

7. *A hardy Japanese azalea.*

The flowers are small but this is no disadvantage, as there are so many of them that the whole bush is covered. They range from white to soft pink through salmon and crimson to red. There are no yellows and there is no scent. They flower in May and June and, like the evergreen rhododendrons, they are happy on the rock garden and in the front of shrub borders. But these are not, by any means, the only uses for the Japanese azaleas and, again like the dwarf rhododendrons, they may be grown in pots or tubs. They may also be forced into flower for early decoration in the house and later planted in the garden.

But they should not be confused with the florists' azaleas, very different plants, which are dealt with in the next chapter; for, unlike these, the Japanese azaleas are comparatively hardy, Give them a light sprinkling of straw or bracken among the branches in the winter until they are 18 in. high and 18 in. through. This applies only to the colder, drier parts of the country. Where the humidity is high, it will not be so important, neither will it be when the frosts are less severe—but these two conditions often go together.

Four main groups concern us at the moment, until they are more neatly classified by the experts. The first of these are the forms and varieties of *R. indicum*. These were (and often still are) known as *Azalea macrantha*.

Rhododendron indicum varieties   Here I would like to emphasize that these plants have practically no connexion with the florists' azaleas, sometimes wrongly known as '*indicas*' or 'Indian' azaleas, although both may be, and are, grown in pots and used for decoration in the house.

The true *R. indicum* is late flowering, and most of the varieties are salmon-pink and salmon-red with a touch of orange in some forms. All of these, and the forms of *R. macrostemnon*, which are similar, flower in June and July.

This *indica/macrostemnon* group is not the most important although it is not the least attractive. I mention it first because it is the one that is most often confused wih the greenhouse azaleas in name.

Kurume Azaleas The largest group of all is the 'Kurume' section. These varieties come from *R. obtusum* or, as it is still popularly known, *Azalea amoena*. There are hundreds of different sorts, mostly from Japan. There are many natural hybrids and countless that have been man-made, in Japan, in Holland, in the United States of America and in this country. *R. obtusum* itself is very hardy, but some are inclined to scorn it for its colour—rich magenta. This is a pity, because it is one of the most reliable of all and the form of the shrub is attractive for all the year—I find the flowers more than charming.

Recently, *Azalea* (*Rhododendron*) *kaempferi* has been placed in this group although it was once thought to be a separate species on its own. It is certainly different from *Rhododendron obtusum*. It is taller, sometimes reaching 5 or 6 ft. in woodland. The flowers are large, but fewer, and the colour can best be described as salmon to orange-red—but there are different forms, with almost all shades from pink to scarlet. This has been crossed with a species named *R. malvatica* to give a most useful race of hybrid azaleas of medium habit (reaching about 4 ft.)

with semi-evergreen foliage (those leaves that fall turn colour before they do) and with large flowers in shades from pink to brick-red, larger than the Kurumes but equally well displayed. These are known as the *mal-vatica* × *kaempferi* hybrids and all are excellent garden plants.

This is only an outline of the principal groups of dwarf hardy evergreen azaleas grown today in this country. A short list of suggested varieties is given in Chapter Nine. Wonderful new sorts are being raised in the United States of America. The most outstanding of these are the Glenn Dale azaleas which combine the hardiness of the Kurumes and their allies with the size of flower of the *R. (A.) simsii* hybrids, the greenhouse or florists or 'Indian' azaleas, dealt with in the next chapter.

CHAPTER FIVE

DWARF EVERGREEN INDOOR AZALEAS

Rhododendron simsii At the same time as the 'Swamp
Honeysuckle' (*Rhododendron* (*Azalea*) *viscosum*) was introduced into England, *R.* (*Azalea*) *simsii*, then wrongly
known as *A. indica* was introduced into Holland. *R.
simsii* is much more tender than *R. indicum*, but the
flowers are much larger. Years later, in 1843 to be exact,
another variety, *R.* (*A.*) *simsii* var. *vittatum*, was introduced into Belgium. This was hybridized with the original
species and a number of seedlings were raised.

Hybrids That, to say the least, is putting it mildly.
Millions were raised and thousands were named—for the
greenhouse azalea was fashionable in the nineteenth century. It was used for decorating ballrooms and drawing-
rooms, either in its natural state or twisted and tormented,
in the fashion of the time, into curious shapes. Strangely
enough, it was not one of the new seedlings that was the
most outstanding of all, but a branch sport (a shoot or
branch that is different in character from the rest of the
plant). This occurred, by the greatest good fortune, on the
nursery of M. Joseph Vervaene of Ghent. This plant is
still as popular today, with its large frilled salmon flowers
spotted red, as it was when it was first introduced one
hundred years ago. It is called after the man who found
the original branch on one of his plants—*Azalea vervaeneana*.

I could go on for pages about these azaleas, about their history and their breeding, the industry in Belgium, their effect on gardening in England, the method of growing, and various tricks, old and new, of forcing and preserving the flowers. But when it was all written it would not add up to much of practical value. What is of real importance is the method of preserving the plants from one winter to the next. So I propose to go away from the general pattern of this book and to give, here and now, the method of caring for the indoor azaleas after they have flowered.

Culture As with all rhododendrons and azaleas, the flowers must be removed as soon as they are over. The plants must then be kept protected from the frost until the risk of frost is past (date depends on local conditions). After this they must be plunged out in a shaded border (the ideal is the north side of a wall) where they must still be kept watered and sprayed. Every third year they should be removed from the pots, the outer ball of root should be shaken out and then they should be repotted in a mixture of peat and sand. They should be taken into the greenhouse before the first frost (date regulated as for the last) and forced according to taste and the facilities of the greenhouse. This method has proved successful in keeping some of these plants for twenty years, during which time they have flowered regularly.

Incidentally, the same treatment may be given to the Kurumes and the *malvatica* × *kaempferi* hybrids, except that it will not be possible to force them into flower so early. Against this is the fact that when they have grown too big for their pots they may be planted out in the

33

garden permanently with safety. The varieties of *R. simsii* will not grow easily in the open garden.

To return to the indoor azaleas for a variety and to the Kurumes for a colour, I should like to mention a striking example of the fatuity of the general aversion to magenta. I remember seeing in a Royal Academy Exhibition, about 1950, a picture entitled 'Princess Beatrix on the Mantelpiece'. Now *Azalea* Princess Beatrix is a rich salmon, touching red, but it was backed, as if freshly bought, by a piece of tissue paper of the kind used by florists, of the same mauve-magenta shade as that of some forms of *Azalea amoena*—the father and mother of all the Kurumes. And if that colour combination can win a place by art in the Royal Academy, then surely we should not scorn to use the same combination of colours by nature in our gardens. For two hardy varieties to give this effect, I would suggest *A.* Anny (a *malvatica* × *kaempferi*, fairly early flowering) and *A. amoena*.

CHAPTER SIX

RHODODENDRON SPECIES

A SPECIES of any plant is a group of individuals that have the same constant and distinctive characters. There are many hundreds of different species of rhododendron, from the humble, work-a-day *ponticum* to the lordly *griffithianum*—both these two having played a large part in the development of the hybrid rhododendron that is most widely grown today.

The division of any plant into species is a convenient way of classifying its natural representatives found growing in the wild. Because there are so many different species of rhododendron, it has been found convenient to group them into series and subseries. These groups have been made according to their botanical and geographical differences and similarities. The geographical aspect is that usually applied to plants in the way that the various types of flowers grow in different parts of the world according to climate and situation. That is to say, it is a matter of position, not nationality. Species belonging to the same series have been found in India, Burma, Tibet and China. There are only two (apart from the enormous Azalea series) that cover the whole world—the *ponticum* and *lapponicum* series have representatives growing in the United States of America, Spain, Portugal, the U.S.S.R. and as far east as the island of Yakusima in Japan.

It is impossible to give a general description of the

species of rhodendron. There are one or two—particularly the dwarf varieties—which may be grown under practically any conditions. But most of the best require a soil and site a little above the average—moist, well-drained soil, light woodland, preferably on slightly rising

8. *A species rhododendron of the macabeanum series.*

ground; comparative freedom from frost is desirable for many and, most important of all, a moist atmosphere.

To find the best way to make a short selection of species, to describe as many as possible without omitting too many of the most important, I have hit on the plan of taking you for a brief, imaginary tour of the Rhododendron Show. The show is usually held in the first week of May, three weeks before the Chelsea Flower Show, at the Royal Horticultural Society's Hall, at Vincent Square, Westminster. Naturally, as a rhododendron specialist, it is the show of shows for me, but it is true to say that it is international, democratic and that it appeals to young and old. There are always many visitors from overseas, particularly from the United States of America and from Holland. As an example of the democratic side of the show, I can remember seeing specimens being brought in for staging in the official vases in all sorts of different containers ranging from champagne bottles (Moët et Chandon, 1947) to milk-bottles (Pasteurized T.T.).

Sooner or later, if you grow a rhododendron, you will go to the show. If your appetite has been whetted enough to do this I hope that you may find that the following notes will add to your enjoyment—for I found, on my first visit, that the Latin names were Greek to me. (For this reason, I have added the English meaning of the names, taken from *The Rhododendron Handbook* of the Royal Horticultural Society.)

Let us, then, produce our Fellow's ticket or pay the cost of admission, and examine some of the high-lights.

Rhododendron arboreum Beginning at the first two or three classes, we shall find a number of different collections of species of rhododendrons. Among these will be many of the finest types and many of the finest blooms that will be in flower over the whole of Great Britain at the time of the show. Somewhere about Class 6, the different competitions will begin for representative blooms of particular species or for different species in a series or subseries. The first that is of interest will be a class for a truss from *Rhododendron arboreum* ('tree-like'). This, as you may remember, is of particular importance because it is the species that gave the colour to the original hybrids. It is rather tender and requires the best possible conditions: it may really be grown only in the south and west or in Scotland and Ireland, where the Gulf Stream softens the climate. There are one or two forms that are more hardy than others, and we may well see *cinnamom-eum* ('cinnamon coloured', referring to the underside of the leaves), a white form with a black spot. If you happen to grow the hybrid rhododendron Sappho (tall, white, with a black spot) you will notice a family likeness. Among those that are tender, but particularly beautiful, there may be a truss of *R. kingianum*, the brightest possible red and with leaves the glossiest dark green.

Rhododendron falconeri As I have space to describe only a selection, let us move on to somewhere around Class 12, where we shall see representatives of trusses of *R. falconeri* (after Hugh Falconer of the Saharanpur Gardens, India, 1832). This is one of the magnificent large-leaved species and, although it is a little more hardy than arboreum, it does need good conditions. However, it might well be tried out in any warm garden inland. Notice the leaves, which are large and leathery, and the enormous truss of yellow flowers—particularly striking with the purple blotch at the base of the flower and the pugnacious quality of the stigma.

The Lacteum series If you happen to feel particularly taken with *falconeri* but think your conditions may not be quite good enough, let us move along quickly to somewhere around Class 19 and find the class for 'Any Rhododendron of the *lacteum* ("milky") series' and see if there is a truss of *R. wightii* (after Robert Wight, one time superintendent of Madras Botanic Garden). Although this is in a different series it also has large yellow flowers and leathery leaves—it could be called the 'poor man's' *falconeri*.

Rhododendron griffithianum I am sorry to have jumped you ahead, because in passing you may have noticed the star of the show—the class numbered around 15 and for blooms of *R. griffithianum* (after William Griffith, one time superintendent of Calcutta Botanic Garden). This one is really a bit difficult to grow and, strictly speaking, should be covered by a greenhouse and the next chapter. I want you to be sure to see it, because it is one that has played a large part in the development of rhododendrons and in making them so outstandingly attractive.

The Fortunei series Having passed the star of the show, we come now to the front row of the chorus—a class described as 'any Rhododendron of the *fortunei* (after Robert Fortune) series other than *griffithianum*', you will find this to be somewhere around Class 16. This will probably include some examples of *R. fortunei*, found by Robert Fortune in Western China just over a hundred years ago. It has good texture to the petal, creamy white flowers and a faint but delicate scent. This species could be grown in most gardens of the British Isles. There may also be representative blooms of *decorum* ('ornamental') —a species similar to *fortunei* but not quite so hardy, yet with a little more colour to the flower. An important member of this series that will not be seen is *R. discolor* ('of various colours')—very late flowering and somewhat similar to *fortunei* in colour and shape of flower, the chief difference, apart from the later flowering period, is that it is taller. There will probably be some sprays and blooms from *R. calophytum* ('beautiful plant') and *R. sutchuenense* (from Szechwan). Personally, I do not think highly of the flowers of these plants but they both have bold leaves and they make impressive bushes. They are also hardy in most parts of the British Isles. The other interesting species (from a possible thirty-four) are *orbiculare* ('circular'—alluding to the leaves) and *fargesii* (after Père Paul Farges of the French missions to China).

Haematodes and Neriiflorum subseries We should now look at the two classes for blooms of species that are classified under the *haematodes* ('blood-like') and *neriiflorum* ('with flowers like oleander') subseries—probably around Classes 23 and 24. The first is the more hardy of the two, but both species and many others represented will have brilliant red flowers of shiny texture, although *haematodes* may be the only one that it will be safe to try to grow. These two classes and the next two contain many species that may well have an influence on rhododendrons of the future. Hybrids raised from these may give a more brilliant colouring, a different form of flower and compact bushy growth, making excellent plants for the smaller garden. Even if some of them might be difficult to grow, we should remember that rhododendrons *arboreum* and *griffithianum* are far from easy yet they have exercised an influence on the hardy hybrid rhododendrons equalled only by that of *R. catawbiense* (from Catawba, North Carolina), the mauve species, from the United States, which will stand 60° F. of frost.

Rhododendron campylocarpum The yellow-flowered rhododendrons, either hybrids or species, are only just beginning to come out of the curio category. Somewhere around Classes 28 and 29 will be found the competition for sprays of flowers of *R. campylocarpum* ('with bent fruits'). This is the yellow-flowered species that has been responsible for most of the yellow-flowered hybrids. Others have been raised from *R. wightii* of the *lacteum* series and *R. wardii* (after F. Kingdon Ward, the collector) and *litiense* (from the Li-ti-ping, Yunnan), both of the *souliei* (after Père J. A. Soulie) subseries of the *thomsonii* (after Thomas Thomson of the Calcutta Botanic Garden) series. *R. campylocarpum* was introduced into this country from the Himalayas at the same time as *R. griffithianum*. For some reason or other, it did not have an immediate influence in the same way. It was only really between the wars that the yellow rhododendron was acknowledged to be an accomplished fact and a free and easy plant for practically any garden with acid soil. It will be interesting to see the sprays of *R. campylocarpum* in the competition, there are two forms—a short compact bush with clear yellow flowers known as 'Hooker's variety' and a taller shrub with yellow flowers touched with vermilion known as variety *elatum*. Both these two may be tried in any reasonably warm garden where other rhododendrons may be grown.

The Souliei subseries Obviously, *R. campylocarpum* is an important species if only for its yellow colouring. For this reason it is given a class by itself in the show. But, in fact, it is a member of the *thomsonii* series and we move on to another section of that series—the *souliei* subseries (this will probably be around Class 31). There are many interesting plants that qualify for this class—*croceum* ('yellow') from Yunnan: *litiense*—another yellow, sometimes blotched: *souliei* itself, pink, saucer-shaped flowers: *wardii* with saucer-shaped yellow flowers with a bright crimson blotch, and last of all, least in size, but almost the loveliest, *williamsianum* (after J. C. Williams), a dwarf grower with heart-shaped leaves, bronze young foliage and flowers that are cups of clear pink.

The Thomsonii subseries The next class will almost certainly be for flowers from plants of the *thomsonii* subseries of the *thomsonii* series (both *campylocarpum* and *souliei* give their names to subseries within the *thomsonii* series). The species *thomsonii* will provide the greater number of exhibits in this class. It needs a sheltered position, but could be grown in gardens in many parts of the country where this can be provided. It is one of the earliest Himalayan rhododendrons to have been introduced (1849) and the leaves are attractive, and the flowers are brilliant—blood-red bells: one of its more beautiful features may not be apparent at the show—the light brown bark with a silver sheen.

The Azalea series It was in 1793 that it was first proposed that azaleas should be called rhododendrons. So it is no new thing to find the next three classes are devoted to the azalea series of the rhododendron. There will be a separate class for the *schlippenbachii* (after Baron von Schlippenbach) series. In this class will be flowers from a plant that may be grown anywhere in the British Isles— *R. reticulatum* ('net-like'). This is a hardy shrub and very attractive. Notice the flat shape of the flower, which is wide open; it is early flowering and stands up to a great deal of frost. The shape of the leaves, which will not yet be developed, is also attractive and unusual. In the class for any deciduous rhododendrons of the azalea series other than *R. schlippenbachii*, we may see practically anything. Probably one of the most outstanding exhibits in this section is *R. vaseyi* (after G. S. Vasey, who discovered this species in North Carolina)—again hardy and with delicate pink-shaded flowers of unusual shape and delightful perfume. The old common azalea (*Azalea pontica*), correctly known as *R. luteum* (yellow), would not be out of place among these more glamorous beauties because it is a first-class garden plant. It has been honoured by the Royal Horticultural Society with the much-coveted Award of Garden Merit.

The Dwarfs Now we skip a few classes and move on to the dwarfs—the classes usually numbered from 41 down to 47. I will not describe these, as many of them are mentioned in the chapter on dwarf evergreen rhododendrons. If you are looking to see the type of plant that belongs to the rhododendron family under this heading you will find them about this position in the show. Incidentally, it is worth having a look to see if there are any representatives of *forrestii*, which is the correct name for *repens* ('creeping') and, as a matter of interest and curiosity, to see *spinuliferum* ('bearing spines')—one of the medium-growing rhododendrons and the one that I had in mind when I mentioned a pincushion shape with pins. Before you start to look round on your own and discover the other species and learn a little about them, we must look at the various classes that come in the *triflorum* ('three-flowered') series. In the section for blooms of *R. augustinii* (after Augustine Henry, sometime Professor of Forestry, Dublin) we shall see some of the best blues that are found in rhododendrons. This plant should not be attempted unless you have a warm garden with woodland. There are some paler forms that are more hardy, but I do not think that it is worth troubling with these unless you can grow the best. Probably the most hardy of all the triflorum subseries (somewhere around Class 52) is *R. ambiguum* ('doubtful'). This is a strange plant and the strangeness is indicated in the name—different specimens of the same plant will sometimes have flowers of yellow and sometimes flowers of purple. The two forms together can make a delightful mixture. A very beautiful yellow rhododendron of this kind is *R. lutescens* ('becoming yellow'), but it is particularly tender and difficult; yet for anyone with a warm garden and suitable conditions it is a distinguished shrub.

The Yunnanense subseries Around Class 53 you will find the entries for 'Any rhododendrons of the *yunnanense* ('from Yunnan') subseries'. Among these will be *R. yunnanense* itself and *R. davidsonianum* (after Dr W. H. Davidson). These are delightfully graceful shrubs. They grow with long slender branches that are covered with small but decorative flowers in white flushed with pink, sometimes attractively spotted. Again, for the best results, they need woodland, moisture and lack of wind and frost. Without these conditions they can be, as a friend of mine once put it, 'scruffy'.

This is just a brief guide to the highlights of the species in the show. You will see many more species, and the hybrid section or the groups have not been mentioned. I hope that this may be enough to help you to enjoy the show and to grow some of the plants. When you want further knowledge I suggest that you buy *The Rhododendron Handbook* of the Royal Horticultural Society and the *Rhododendron Year Books* that are issued each year.

The Auriculatum series I think that I must mention two species that form one series that cannot possibly be at the show because they are so late flowering. These are *R. auriculatum* ('eared': referring to the lobes at the base of the leaves) and *R. griersonianum* (after R. G. Grierson, helper of George Forrest), forming the *auriculatum* series. *R. auriculatum* is a tall-growing tree with large white flowers in August, and *R. griersonianum* is a scrub bush with brilliant geranium-scarlet flowers in June and July. And we should not forget the *ponticum* series, with tough old *catawbiense* that gives us most of the hardiness, and the glamorous *yakusimanum*, with its delicate flowers and felt-cover foliage that may well be the rhododendron of the future.

Returning to the show, there are many classes for rhododendrons of other types and there are two that may interest you if you are a beginner and a coming expert. One is a novices' class for species and the other a novices' class for hybrids. These are open only to people who have never won a prize at the Rhododendron Show before. I hope, perhaps, to make your acquaintance on the day before the show when you are staging your first exhibit.

CHAPTER SEVEN

RHODODENDRONS FOR THE
WARM GARDEN AND THE GREENHOUSE

THIS is a short chapter for the record—and for the interest of the expert of the future.

Rhododendrons for the West Coast Some rhododendrons—a few already described—are almost beyond imagination in beauty, but they need the warmth and moisture of Cornwall or those parts of Wales and Scotland that are lapped by the warm waves of the Gulf Stream. *Griffithianum* is one, *nuttallii* (large leaves, large yellow flowers with scent, in fact the largest flowers of all) is another; *eriogynum* (brilliant red) and *maddenii* (tubular white flowers, also scented) are two more to complete a short selection. These are all straightforward rhododendrons of normal shrub or small-tree habit, similar to all the others, except that they must be wet and warm.

The next group may, on rare occasions and in rare circumstances, be grown out of doors in the wettest and warmest places. They are represented by *R. edgeworthii*, others in that series, and a number of hybrids. The characteristics are large open flowers, usually white with a flush of pink, and all the perfumes of Arabia in each. The leaves are hairy, deep veined, different.

The big thing about the cultivation of these and the next group is that they are partly epiphytic—that is, they grow on other plants but they do not take their nourishment from them (like mistletoe), neither are they climbers (like ivy), neither do they root in the air (like orchids). The result is that both these two groups of rhododendrons are best grown in pots, without too much room for the roots, and with some support for the branches.

Javanese Rhododendrons The last group are definite indoor greenhouse plants, known as the Javanese rhododendrons. The species are *javanicum, brookeanum, jasminiflorum* and a few more. The hybrids from these were many and various, but are not now easily obtainable. They can be grown to provide flowers in every month of the year in every colour of the rainbow and all with a sultry jungle perfume. The great year for the Javanese rhododendrons was 1897, when the fine old firm of Veitch exhibited flowers from them every fortnight at the Royal Horticultural Society's meetings in London.

Once the greenhouse was all-important: more recently natural gardening pushed it into the background. Now, once again it is coming to the front, smaller, cheaper, more tightly packed with interest. Which makes these two last groups of tender species and varieties dual-purpose greenhouse plants for the rhododendron enthusiast and rhododendrons for the enthusiastic greenhouse owner.

No separate list is given for this chapter. In addition to those mentioned, *fragrantissimum* and Countess of Haddington are good hybrids of the second group, and Ne plus Ultra and King Edward VII of the third, but very scarce.

CHAPTER EIGHT

FIRST CROSSES AND
BLUE-BLOODED RHODODENDRONS

THERE are few records of how many of the present range of hardy hybrids were first raised, and fewer still of the ancestry of the later varieties, many of which are the finest plants of the whole race. Soon after the 1914–1918 war there was a new approach to the culture of rhododendrons. Several new species had been introduced and these seemed to open up a wide field for the hybridist. To encourage this work, the Rhododendron Association was formed under the enthusiastic leadership of the late Mr Lionel de Rothschild. The Association published its first *Year Book* in 1929, and in 1932 it was proposed that a '*Stud Book*' should be included. This suggestion was approved subject to the following rules: 1. All first crosses (hybrids between two species) should be entered. 2. All hybrids which had received an Award of Merit or a First Class Certificate should also be included—where the parentage was known. 3. All crosses between two hybrids already in the *Stud Book* or crosses between a registered hybrid and a species should also be eligible for entry in the *Stud Book*.

This *Stud Book* has been carried on in the *Rhododendron Handbook* of the Royal Horticultural Society. The rules are more or less the same, except that they have been slightly relaxed so far as the third condition is concerned;

a hybrid may now be included even if only one parent is a species and the breeding of the other parent is unknown. The conditions have been slightly tightened, however, to limit the list to hybrids whose names have been registered with the International Registrar for Rhododendrons. The list of hybrids of known parentage has now risen from 246, in 1934, to well over 1,000 in the latest edition of the *Rhododendron Handbook*. No doubt many more will be included in the next and later editions. And when these become obtainable from nurseries they are added to the list of hybrids usually available (this list also contains most of the hardy hybrids).

First Crosses The simplest way to demonstrate the working of the *Stud Book* is to take one or two examples. The classic first cross between two species is *R. loderi*— *R. griffithianum* × *R. fortunei*, raised by the late Sir Edmund Loder in 1907. *Griffithianum* is a tender plant of magnificent flower, slightly scented: *fortunei* is much more hardy, with a flower that is rather smaller but of fine texture. The resulting cross produces a moderately hardy rhododendron of fine foliage, immense flowers and delicate scent. Not entirely hardy, it is suitable for only the more favoured gardens. Even so, it is the outstanding example of a first cross between two species. It is also an example of the need for the registration of names. The same cross was made at Kew Gardens in 1888 and different forms of this rhododendron, that had been named '*kewense*', and different forms of '*loderi*' are similar in appearance.

Hybrids of Mixed Ancestry The finest example of a

rhododendron of mixed ancestry that has received an Award of Merit is *R*. Countess of Derby. The parents were *R*. Pink Pearl and *R*. Cynthia; it was raised by the late Mr Harry White in 1913. Now the parentage of Pink Pearl is only assumed to be *R. broughtonii* crossed with *R*. George Hardy (thought to be a hybrid between *R. catawbiense* and *R. griffithianum*). The parentage of Cynthia is lost in the mists of antiquity. But the resulting cross is well worth its entry in the *Stud Book*—it can hold its own with any high-bred hybrid. The flower is a most attractive shade of pink, it is large, the truss is well formed and the foliage is stout.

An old example of a rhododendron that is a cross between a species and a hybrid entered in the *Stud Book* is *R. jacksonii*. This most useful early-flowering, bushy-growing rhododendron, with pink flowers striped with red, is the result of hybridizing *R. caucasicum* with *R. nobleanum*. Now this gives an added proportion of *caucasicum* blood, because *nobleanum* is a cross between *R. arboreum* and *R. caucasicum*. The result is that *jacksonii* is more hardy, more bushy, a little later to flower and not quite so highly coloured as some of the forms of *R. nobleanum*. A more modern example would be *R*. Blue Diamond, a hybrid between *R*. Intrifast (dwarf and purple) and *R. augustinii* (tall and blue). This makes Blue Diamond the plant that we would expect—a bushy compact shrub with near-blue flowers. Intrifast is a hybrid between *R. intricatum* and *R. fastigiatum*—hence the name.

An example of the later ruling on the parentage required to qualify for inclusion in the *Stud Book* is *R.* Vulcan, one of the few moderately successful hybrids of *R. griersonianum*. It is a cross between that species and one of the more modern hardy hybrids, *R.* Mars. *R. griersonianum* is a staggering plant of intense scarlet colour, late flowering. It is rather straggly and a little tender. Mars is a compact hardy hybrid with deep red flowers. The resulting plant is brilliant in colour and of reasonable habit.

R. griersonianum is probably one of the best species for the beginner to use in hybridization. Although no really successful hybrid has yet been produced from this species, it has the advantage of begetting plants that flower young. With some of the other species it is necessary to wait as long as fifteen years before they flower. Not so with *griersonianum* hybrid seedlings, which produce flowers within four or five years and, under favourable conditions, sometimes sooner.

This brief guide will act, I hope, as a stimulant to encourage you to hybridize and raise a new rhododendron yourself. (*See* Chapter Fourteen.) But remember, if you raise a new rhododendron it is only one plant that should be named, and not the whole race of seedlings grown as the result of your cross. You should wait to see every plant flower, as there will be many variations even in a cross between two pure species. Choose and name only the best.

CHAPTER NINE

SELECT LISTS OF RHODODENDRONS

SELECT LIST OF HARDY HYBRID RHODODENDRONS

(*See* Chapter One)

KEY

The flowering season is indicated by the approximate period during which the flowers open, as follows:

VE—Very early	(Christmas to April)
E—Early	(April to beginning of May)
EM—Early mid-season	(mid-May)
M—Mid-season	(end of May)
L—Late	(June)
VL—Very late	(June to July)

The habit of the plant is shown by the following letters:

C—Compact, growing to 3 to 3½ ft. × 3 to 4 ft.

M—Medium   „   „ 4 to 5 ft. × 3 to 4 ft.

T—Tall   „   „ 6 to 7 ft. × 3 to 4 ft.

All the above measurements to be attained in approximately seven to eight years, under average garden conditions from an 18-in. plant.

The hardiness is shown:

A—hardy anywhere in the British Isles and may be planted in full exposure if desired.

B—hardy anywhere in the British Isles but requires some shade to obtain the best results.

B(S)—hardy anywhere in the British Isles but requires some shade owing to the lateness of the flower, which may burn in hot sunlight.

(Letters show—season, habit, hardiness, in that order)

Alice Rose-pink flowers rising in a tall truss; erect growth. M.M.B.

Ascot Brilliant Blood-red bells; rounded leaves on red wood. E.M.B.

Bagshot Ruby Ruby-red flowers; good foliage, also on red wood. M.M.B(S).

B. de Bruin Dark red; a little loose. L.T.A.

Betty Wormald Lavish flowers, pink with overtones; strong leaves and growth. M.M.B.

Britannia A loose truss of gloxinia-shaped, near-scarlet flowers; leaves are naturally yellow, adding charm to the colour of the flower. M.C.B(S).

Chevalier Felix de Sauvage Crimson with a dark eye, very striking; bushy and spreading. E.C.B.

Christmas Cheer Pink, small trusses but many of them; a trim figure. VE.C.B.

Chionoides Neat flower, white with a yellow eye, narrow leaves, wide plant. L.C.A.

Countess of Athlone Large mauve; good leaves. EM.M.A.

Countess of Derby Flower upon flower of rich pink, strong leaves, strong growth. M.M(almost T.)A.

Cunningham's White Yellow centre; extra-tough, for smoky districts. E.C.A.

Cynthia Rosy crimson; reliable, resilient. EM.M.A.

Diphole Pink Rich pink of unusual shade; dark green leaves. L.M.A.

Duchess of Teck Rose-pink flowers with yellow centre; upturned dark green leaves. VL.M.A.

Earl of Donoughmore Glowing scarlet; light yellow-green leaves. M.M.B.

Eileen Tall truss in rose-pink shaded deeper; good dark leaves and habit. L.M.A.

Elsa Crisp Pink with a deeper edge; good habit and foliage. M.M.B.

Fastuosum fl. pl. Semi-double rosettes of mauve, holds leaf well. M.M.A.

General Eisenhower Big flowers of rich red; long leaves and strong growth. L.T.A.

George Hardy Pink buds fading to pure white; narrow. E.M.T.B.

Goldsworth Orange Pale orange, an unripe Jaffa; interesting when out of flower. VL.C.B(S).

Goldsworth Yellow Pale yellow, pink buds; foliage may burn in sun. EM.M.B.

Gomer Waterer Blush, fading to white; dark green leaves. L.M.A.

Handsworth White Coloured as the name; geometrically patterned habit. E.C.B.

Hon. J. M. Montague Waxy scarlet, glowing; dark green leaves. EM.M.B.

Jacksonii Pink with a deeper stripe; leaves may burn until well established, but do not worry. E.C.A.

Kluis Sensation Scarlet-red with almost a suggestion of

orange; dark leaves well held on green wood. VL.C.B(S).

Kluis Triumph Glowing red petals of good texture; compact habit. M.C.B.

Lady Annette de Trafford A delicate shade of pink with a dark eye; rotund, with light green leaves. VL.C.A.

Lady Clementine Mitford Pink with a yellow centre giving a peach effect; young growth silver. L.M.A.

Lady Decies Mauve, yellow centre; tall and strong. L.T.A.

Madame de Bruin A fine scarlet-red; upright. EM.M.A.

Michael Waterer Rich red; narrow leaves but plenty of them. L.M.B(S).

Midsummer Very late pink with a yellow eye; apt to be loose. VL.T.A.

Moser's Maroon Rich maroon-red; brilliant young foliage. VL.T.A.

Mother of Pearl There is no better description; foliage same as Pink Pearl. M.M.A.

Mrs Furnival Pink with well-defined red blotch; rounded habit. M.M.A.

Mrs G. W. Leak Soft pink, red blotch spreading to the petal; well shaped. EM.M.B.

Mrs R. S. Holford Salmon-pink, almost the only one; light green leaves. VL.M.A.

Mrs T. Lowinsky Orchid-shaped flower of ivory-white with orange flare; always looks well. L.M.A.

Mrs William Agnew Deep pink edge, pink in the centre, yellow blotch; strong and vigorous. VL.T.A.

Mum White flowers with a yellow eye; comfortable habit and foliage. VL.C.A.

Nobleanum Pink to crimson; the variety that often flowers at Christmas. VE.C.B.

Old Port Colour is described by the name; a reliable grower. M.M.A.

Pierre Moser Star-shaped pink flowers; occasionally unruly, check with pruning. E.T.A.

Pink Pearl Pink flowers with deeper buds; foliage can be a foot long. EM.M.A.

Praecox Many small rich mauve flowers; scented foliage. VE.C.B.

Purple Splendour Rich and dark—but frilled edge adds glamour; dark glossy leaves. M.M.A.

Souvenir de D. A. Koster Rich red flowers of unusual shape; red wood, good strong leaves. VL.C.B(S).

Souvenir de Dr S. Endtz Deep pink; good bushy grower. M.M.A.

The Bride White with green spots; light green leaves. EM.C.A.

Trilby Dark red with darker spots; red wood, long leaves. M.M.A.

Zuider Zee Large yellow; light leaves and upright growth. EM.M.B.

A SELECTION OF DWARF RHODODENDRONS

(See Chapter Two)

(It is not easy to list the dwarfs with a simple key. Most of them flower at the end of April or early May, only exceptions to this are noted. Most may be grown anywhere and exceptions are marked W indicating that generally they like it wet and warm—these should not be attempted where conditions are very cold or very dry. The ultimate height is given for the open, in not too rich a soil.)

Blue Diamond (hybrid between Intrifast and *augustinii*) Electric blue, free flowering. 3 ft.

Blue Tit (hybrid between *impeditum* and *augustinii*) Blue, light green foliage; young growth almost golden. 2 to 3 ft.

calostrotum (species of the Saluenense series) Flat magenta flowers; leaves covered in light down. 15 in.

Creeping Jenny (hybrid between *griersonianum* and *forrestii*: form of Elizabeth) Red flowers: trailing habit. 9 to 12 in. high, 4 ft. in length. W.

Elizabeth (hybrid between *griersonianum* and *repens*) Very free flowering, intense red; attractive young foliage. 3 ft. W.

fastigiatum (species of the Lapponicum series) Light purple flowers in plenty; dwarf but erect growth. 15 to 18 in.

ferrugineum (species of the Ferrugineum series) 'The Alpine Rose'. Rosy crimson; leaves rusty beneath. *R. hirsutum* is closely allied and said to be the most tolerant of lime. June flowering. 2 to 3 ft.

impeditum (species of the Lapponicum series) Purple-blue flowers; small leaves. 12 in.

keleticum (species of the Saluenense series) Purple saucers; green leaves, silvery underneath. 9 in.

pemakoense (species of the Uniflorum series) Comparatively large flowers in shades of purple; the only evergreen rhododendron to spread by suckers. 12 in. W.

racemosum (species of the Virgatum series) Pink; red
wood, green leaves, white beneath. 3 ft.

russatum (species of the Lapponicum series) The best
purple; a little taller than very dwarf. 15 to 24 in.

williamsianum (species of the Williamsianum subseries
of the Thomsonii series) Clear pink, cup-shaped
flowers; heart-shaped leaves, bronze young growth.
12 in. Slightly W.

A SELECTION OF DECIDUOUS AZALEAS
(See Chapter Three)

(No key is given for the hybrids—a general description is
given of the habits of each type: species described in
full.)

Species.

luteum (better known as *Azalea pontica*) Rich yellow
flowers, beautifully scented; May; tall, reaches 7 to
8 ft. in time; good autumn foliage.

luteum var. glauca As above, with glaucous foliage.

reticulatum Open flowers of crimson, distinct shape;
early May; square-cut diamond-shaped leaves;
medium.

vaseyi Tubular buds opening to cups of pale pink with
faint red spots; early May; pointed leaves; medium.

viscosum Long white flowers, very strongly scented;
July and August; slightly glaucous leaves; tall.

Ghent Azaleas—a short selection Flowering at the end of May or early June. Many are well scented and some have good autumn colour. Except where otherwise stated, they are moderately tall growing, reaching 5 ft. in ten years under normal garden conditions from an average plant sent out by a grower.

Altaclarense Sunbeam Bright yellow, orange blotch, large flower and truss, scented; good autumn colour; wide grower.

Bouquet de flore Pink striped white, scented; tall; autumn colour.

coccinea speciosa Brilliant orange-red, prominent stamens.

daviesii Cream, yellow flare, wonderful perfume; late; glaucous foliage.

Gloria Mundi Bright orange, yellow flare; compact.

Grandeur Triumphans Violet-red; tall.

Josephine Klinger Salmon-pink, yellow lobe.

Nancy Waterer Golden yellow, deep yellow eye, scented; autumn colour.

Norma Double deep pink, scented (strictly a member of the group known as *rustica fl. pl.*)

Raphael de Smet Pale pink, deepening at base of flower, scented, double; compact; autumn colour.

Unique Predominantly orange; tall.

Mollis Azaleas (including *mollis, mollis × sinensis* and *molle-japonicum* hybrids) Flowering during the early part of May with large individual flowers before the leaves are formed. There is little scent to the flowers, but the young foliage has an attractive bitter-sweet aroma. They are medium-growing, bushy plants reaching 3½ to 4 ft. under normal garden conditions from an average plant sent out by a grower.

Seedlings Most nurseries supply unnamed seedlings of the Mollis azaleas in a good range of colour with the accent on the salmon-orange or apricot shades. These are very effective for garden decoration and are less expensive than the named varieties.

Named varieties—a short selection:

Babeuff Salmon-orange, early; upright growth.

Chicago Light orange-red.

Comte de Gomer Pink.

Dr M. Oesthoek Rich orange-red; backs of leaves silver.

Dr Reichenbach Light salmon-orange spreading habit.

Hamlet Salmon-orange, deeper, with spots in throat.

Hortulanus Witte Bright yellow; strong grower.

Imperator Light orange, blotched.

J. C. Van Thol Red; tall, narrow growth.

Koster's Brilliant Red Glowing orange-red.

Lemonora Apricot, tinted rose; spreading.

Nicholas Beets Deep orange, touched with red.

Occidentalis Hybrids The buds open at the end of May, the flowers last through June. All are beautifully scented. The chief attraction is the large truss of flower, more prominent than in the foregoing but passed on to the

Knap Hills. Strong growing, reaching 6 to 7 ft. in ten years under normal garden conditions from an average plant sent out by a grower.

Exquisita Cream, flushed pink, orange flare, a large round head (truss) of flower. (Note—Equisita is possibly a little more blotched than the other hybrids but there is little to choose between it and the others with similar names—Delicatissima, Gloriosa, Graciosa, Magnifica and Superba.)

Irene Koster Pink, deeper stripe, very beautifully scented but not quite so large a truss as the other varieties.

Knap Hill Azaleas These combine the best qualities of all of the foregoing. Late flowering (end of May to June), they have a wide range of colour, large individual flowers in large trusses. Often the flowers have distinct shape, as well as size and scent, with attractively prominent stamens. They all colour, to a greater or lesser degree, in the autumn. Moderate height, reaching 4 to 5 ft. in ten years under normal garden conditions from the average plant sent out by a grower. The selection of varieties has been made with difficulty from over 150 named in recent years.

Seedlings Several nurseries offer seedlings of these azaleas—particularly of the Exbury strain. These, as with the Mollis seedlings, are very good for general garden decoration and are less expensive than the named varieties.

Named varieties—a short selection

Bright Forecast Salmon, with orange blotch; bright autumn colour.

Eisenhower A combination of orange and scarlet; upright habit.

Gibraltar Rich orange, large flowers well shaped; bronze-red autumn foliage.

Gog Tangerine-orange, large flowers; fine autumn colour.

Golden Dream Golden yellow, open flowers; mixture of green and bronze; autumn colour.

Golden Oriole Bright yellow; free flowering and vigorous.

Golden Sunset Large primrose-yellow, suffused apricot; bushy grower.

Hiawatha Flame-red, orange blotch; vigorous.

Honeysuckle White flushed pink, orange blotch.

Kathleen Salmon-pink with deep orange blotch; very good autumn colour.

Knap Hill Apricot Apricot-yellow, large truss, scented.

Knap Hill Red Deep but brilliant red; bronze-tinted foliage.

Marionette Pink with orange flash, scented; strong grower.

Peach Blossom Carmine, orange blotch.

Persil Pure white, pale yellow eye.

Pink Lady Apricot-pink, large open flower.

Princess Royal Cream with pale yellow blotch. One of the largest individual flowers.

Royal Command Vermilion-red.

Satan Bright scarlet, one of the best, scented; good autumn foliage (almost identical with Devon).

Silver Slipper White, slightly suffused pink when first open.

Sun Chariot Buttercup yellow, orange blotch on upper lobe.

Toucan Large pale cream, scented; vigorous.

Tunis Scarlet, tinted orange.

Whitethroat Double white; bushy grower.

A SELECTION OF DWARF EVERGREEN
HARDY AZALEAS
(See Chapter Four)

Key

The flowering season is indicated by the following letters:

E—May.
L—End of May, June.

The habit is shown:

C—compact, growing to 18 to 24 in.
M—medium, growing to 3 to 3½ ft.

The above heights to be attained in ten years from the usual size plant sent out by growers.

(No hardiness rating is given, as all varieties are much the same. They may need protection in severe weather until well established.)

For general information, the type is given in brackets

after each variety. M × K = *malvatica* × *kaempferi*. Kur = Kurume. K = *kaempferi* hybrid with some other species. Where no type is given, the plant is a species or a form of a species.

Anny (M × K)   Orange-red; some autumn colour. E.M.

Bengal Fire (K)   Orange-scarlet. L.M.

Daimio (K)   Orange. L.M.

Eddy (K)   Flame-red, spotted. L.M.

Hatsugiri (Kur)   Mauve. E.C.

Hinomayo (Kur)   Shell pink. E.C.

Hinodegiri (Kur)   Red. E.C.

indicum—(also known as *macrantha*)   Salmon. L.C.

indicum var. balsaminaeflora (also known as *rosaeflora*) Salmon, double rose-shaped flowers. L.C.

John Cairns (K)   Red. E.M.

kaempferi   Salmon to scarlet in different forms. L.M.

Kirin (Kur)   Pink, deeper on outer petal; hose in hose (i.e. one flower inside another). E.C.

ledifolia alba—See *mucronatum*.

macrantha—See *indicum*.

mucronatum (formerly known as *ledifolia alba*)   White, grey-green leaves. E.C.

obtusum (also known as *Azalea amoena*)   Magenta; free flowering; neat foliage, good habit. E.C.

obtusum var. coccinea   As above except flowers are red. E.M.

Palestrina (Kur × mollis?)   Pure white, faintly spotted green, very cool and restful. E.M.

rosaeflora—See *indicum* var. *balsaminaeflora*.

Seikei (Kur)   White, hose in hose. E.C.
Willy (M × K)   Pink. L.M.

A SELECTION OF DWARF EVERGREEN
INDOOR AZALEAS
(See Chapter Five)

There are many different varieties available of these azaleas, and most people will choose those that they prefer when buying plants in flower from florists' shops. However, the following list shows the popular varieties under the headings—Early (suitable for Christmas forcing) and Later (Christmas to Easter forcing).

Early

Mde Petrick   Pink.
Th. Findeisen   Red
Perle de Noisy   Pink and White.
Paul Schaeme   Salmon.
Princess Beatrix   Rich salmon.
Eri Schaeme   Salmon-pink and white.

Later

Vervaeneana rosea   Pink and white.
Vervaeneana saumona   Salmon and pink.
Vervaeneana rubra   Dark red.
Avenir   Salmon-red.
Apollo   Brick-red.
Ernest Thiers   Cerise.

A SELECTION OF RHODODENDRON SPECIES
(See Chapter Six)

This section is divided into three sub-sections for gardening purposes. All require light woodland conditions to see them at their best.

Twelve species with a reasonable chance of success anywhere in Great Britain where the soil is acid

ambiguum ('doubtful')   Small to medium size (3 to 4 ft.); small leaves, yellow or mauve flowers. April to May. (Triflorum series.)

argyrophyllum ('with silver leaves')   Medium to large (6 to 15 ft.); slender silver leaves are the chief attraction; flowers white flushed pink. May. (Arboreum series, Argyrophyllum subseries.)

auriculatum ('eared')   Very tall (15 to 20 ft.); big leaves on rather bare stems; flowers large and white. July to August. (Auriculatum series.)

cinnabarinum ('cinnabar red')   Medium (6 to 8 ft.); narrow glaucous leaves; tubular flowers of cinnabar red. May to June. (Cinnabarinum series.)

dichroanthum ('with two-coloured flowers')   Medium size (up to 6 ft.); compact spreading growth; flowers pale orange or salmon. May to June (Neriiflorum series, Sanguineum subseries.)

discolor ('of various colours')   Tall (12 to 15 ft.); upright growth; flowers white or pale pink. July. (Fortunei series.)

fargesii (after Père Paul Farges)   Medium to tall (6 to

15 ft.); slender growth, attractive foliage; flowers bright pink. April. (Fortunei series, Oreodoxa subseries.)

fortunei (after Robert Fortune) Tall (15 ft.); slightly glaucous leaves; pale pink scented flowers of good texture. (Fortunei series.)

haematodes ('blood-like') Small to medium (3 to 4 ft.); neat leaves with down underneath; tubular blood-red flowers. (Neriiflorum series, Haematodes subseries.)

wightii (after Robert Wight) Medium to tall (8 to 18 ft.); large leathery leaves; large yellow flowers with red spot, April. (Lacteum series.)

yakusimanum ('from Yakusima') Bushy (3 ft. by 3 ft.) The most beautiful rhododendron of all—delicate pink flowers, young leaves covered in thick silver fur, hard as iron.

yunnanense ('from Yunnan') Medium to tall (6 to 12 ft.); small leaves on graceful stems; pale pink flowers spotted red; May. (Triflorum series, Yunnanense subseries.)

Six species that like it just a little more wet and warm to look their best

aberconwayi (after Lord Aberconway) Medium (3 to 8 ft.); curving leathery leaves; saucer-shaped flowers, white flushed pink with crimson spots. May. (Irroratum series.)

campylocarpum ('with bent fruits') Small to medium (4 to 8 ft.); small rounded leaves; cup-shaped yellow flowers; April–May. (Thomsonii series, Campylocarpum subseries.)

griersonianum (after R. C. Grierson) Medium to tall (5 to 7 ft.); rather 'scrubby' habit; scarlet flower. July. (Auriculatum series.)

lutescens ('becoming yellow') Small to medium (about 5 ft.); young leaves bronze; yellow flowers with green spots; February to April. (Triflorum series.)

mucronulatum (with a small point') Small to medium (4 to 8 ft.); deciduous; very early flowering—sometimes in January, but reasonably hardy; bright rose-pink. (Dauricum series.)

thomsonii (after Thomas Thomson) Tall (8 to 18 ft.); glaucous rounded leaves on silvery brown stems; waxy, blood-red, bell-shaped flowers; April. (Thomsonii series.)

*Six species that must have the best conditions,
wet and warm*

arboreum var. Kingianum ('tree-like') Very tall (can reach 30 ft.); glossy dark leaves; brilliant red flowers; April. (Arboreum series). (Moves up a group in hardiness if garden reasonably warm.)

augustinii (after Augustine Henry) Tall (8 to 12 ft.); small leaves, aromatic when crushed; best form has deep blue flowers—inferior colours are more hardy. April–May. (Triflorum series, Augustinii subseries.)

eriogynum ('with a woolly ovary') Medium to tall (up to 10 ft.); clear red flowers, late. (Irroratum series, Parishii subseries.)

falconeri (after Hugh Falconer) Tall (up to 50 ft.); wide leaves, red beneath; enormous pale yellow flowers; April–May (Falconerii series). (Moves up a group in hardiness if garden reasonably warm.)

sinogrande (large)   Tall (up to 30 ft.); immense leaves, sometimes 18 in. long; large truss of creamy white flowers; April. (Grande series.)

wardii (after F. Kingdon Ward)   Medium to tall (8 to 15 ft.); rounded leaves; open, cup-shaped flowers of bright yellow; May. (Thomsonii series, Souliei sub-series.) (Moves up a group in hardiness if garden reasonably warm.)

FIRST CROSSES AND BLUE-BLOODED RHODODENDRONS—A SHORT SELECTION
(See Chapter Eight)

All these hybrids need light woodland conditions to be at their best.

Azor (*griersonianum* × *discolor*)   Salmon-pink; late; loose habit; several different forms in varying shades. June to July.

Bonfire ((*discolor* × Mrs R. T. Shaw) × *griersonianum*) Dark red; loose habit. June.

Bow Bells (*Corona* × *williamsianum*)   Pink bells; low growing. April.

Cilpinense (*ciliatum* × *moupinense*)   Many white flowers touched with pink; low growing. March.

Cornubia (*arboreum* × *shilsonii*)   Waxy scarlet open flowers; tall with attractive foliage. April. (Sheltered gardens only.)

David (Hugh Koster × *neriiflorum*) Deep red; good foliage; moderately hardy.

F. C. Puddle (*neriiflorum* × *griersonianum*) Red; medium to small bush. May.

Fabia (*dichroanthum* × *discolor*) Salmon touched with orange; medium size. May to June.

Fusilier (*elliottii* × *griersonianum*) Scarlet; tall growing; large leaves. June. (Sheltered gardens only.)

Hawk (*wardii* × Lady Bessborough) Yellow, large flowers; tall. May. (Sheltered gardens only.)

Lady Bessborough (*discolor* × *campylocarpum* var. *elatum*) Pale yellow, red throat; tall. May to June.

Lady Chamberlain (*cinnabarinum* var *roylei* × Royal Flush (*cinnabarinum* × *maddenii*)) Large tubular flowers in shades of orange and salmon. May. (Sheltered gardens only.)

Letty Edwards (*campylocarpum* var. *elatum* × *fortunei*) Yellow with red spot in throat; good habit. May. Hardy.

Loderi (*griffithianum* × *fortunei*) Pink, large flower and truss; blue-green leaves. May.

Luscombei (*fortunei* × *thomsonii*) Hanging flowers of deep pink; rounded blue-green leaves. Early May. Hardy.

Racil (*racemosum* × *ciliatum*) Mass of small white flowers touched with pink; neat, compact habit. April. Hardy.

Romany Chai (Moser's Maroon × *griersonianum*) Orange-scarlet; loose grower. June. Hardy.

CHAPTER TEN

THE SOIL AND THE SITUATION

THE SOIL

An Acid Soil Required   The main essential about the soil for any rhododendron or any azalea is that it should be acid. There must be no lime or chalk. A soil test will show the acidity of the soil in terms of a symbol called *p*H. The neutral figure is *p*H 7, readings above this figure show increasing alkalinity (or greater amounts of lime), and readings below indicate increasing acidity. Rhododendrons will grow in a soil with a reading of *p*H 6·5, but they prefer those which have a figure of around *p*H 5 or a little lower. If it is not practical or convenient to have the soil tested, the natural vegetation in the surrounding country is a rough guide. If gorse, pine-trees, heather, silver birch, sedge grass are to be found in the wild then it is a clear indication that the soil is acid. The most obvious sign that the soil may be unsuitable is the presence of old man's beard or traveller's joy in the hedgerows. This, combined with viburnums, myrobalan plum, verbascums and yews growing in the wild will show that the natural soil is not right for rhododendrons.

Texture   The texture of the soil is of small importance. It is wrong to think that rhododendrons will not grow in a heavy soil. They will do very well indeed in this type provided that it is acid and does not contain lime.

Moisture Although many varieties, hybrids and species prefer to have a good supply of moisture, it is more dangerous for the soil to be too wet than too dry. Good drainage is essential. The question of a wet or dry soil is difficult, particularly with azaleas. The very word 'azalea' means dry, because *Rhododendron luteum* (*Azalea pontica*), grows naturally in a dry place. Against this is the name of *R. viscosum*, the 'Swamp Honeysuckle', which, as the name indicates, grows in swamps in Virginia. Yet with hybrids containing the blood of each, too much may be worse than too little.

It is important to remember that an acid soil does not mean a poor soil, although poor soils often are acid. A rich acid soil is required because rhododendrons are great feeders.

Preparation Most deficiencies can be made good by preparing the soil. Deep digging, to a depth of two spits, is very important. It is equally important that a wide area should be prepared, even for only one plant. A minimum of 4 ft. by 4 ft. is desirable; it is still better to prepare a big area for several plants, rather than small islands for isolated specimens. The addition of peat, leafmould and well-rotted cow manure to the soil when it is being prepared will be helpful to nearly all varieties. This should not be put too deep, because rhododendrons are surface rooting; if it is below 15 in. they may never enjoy its nourishment. The subsoil should be broken up in order to allow surplus moisture to drain away and, paradoxically, to allow the moisture to rise by capillary attraction in dry weather.

There is one exception to the rule regarding the addition of manure to the soil—the dwarf rhododendrons will not need too rich a mixture, as this would make them grow out of character becoming comparatively tall and a little straggly.

SITUATION

Provided the soil conditions are right, the hardy hybrid rhododendrons and the deciduous azaleas will grow in practically any situation, although some varieties have been described as having a preference for shade; the reason for this is given in the descriptions in the lists in Chapter Nine, but this should not be overdone—too much shade may cause failure to set flower bud. A little shade is an advantage for all azaleas because it helps the flowers to last longer and prevents them being bleached by hot sunlight. It should be mentioned that many hardy hybrid rhododendrons are seen at their best when they are allowed to grow to individual specimens.

The dwarf rhododendrons prefer an open position in full sunlight. If they are grown in too deep shade, they will become straggly and unkempt. However, the dwarf azaleas do not mind so much whether the position is sunny or shady. They will also become taller in the shade but they do not necessarily suffer in appearance. They will grow a little taller and more open but they are none the less beautiful.

The best species and the first crosses and the 'blue-blooded' hybrids need perfect conditions. There are one or two, particularly the species *thomsonii*, that need plenty of moisture. They also need the shade of light woodland—silver birches probably being the perfect protectors. If possible, the ground should be slightly rising so that any cold air will drain away. In spite of the fame of the 'Rhododendron Dell' at Kew Gardens, it can often happen that a hollow is not the most sheltered place; it may be a frost pocket.

Hardiness So far as the general situation throughout the country is concerned, the question of relative degrees of hardiness is often more one of the humidity of the atmosphere than the amount of frost experienced at any one time. For this reason, it is easier to grow some of the more tender species in the midlands than it is within fifty miles of London, where the atmosphere is dry. Similarly, Norfolk, with its suitable soil and moist atmosphere, and any coastal area where the soil is suitable, are all districts where the more tender kinds may be tried with a reasonable hope of success. Needless to say, the south-west of England is suitable for any kind of rhododendron, and any of the areas that are closely affected by the Gulf Stream—North Wales, Southern Ireland, parts of Northern Ireland, the west coast of Scotland. As with the midlands, it is possible to grow the more tender varieties more easily north of Glasgow than it is in the London and Home Counties area.

CHAPTER ELEVEN

PLANTING AND POT CULTURE

Transplanting Rhododendrons may be transplanted up to practically any size. They form fibrous roots which do not become coarse. It takes from five to seven years, according to the variety, to produce a plant size from 15 to 18 in. high by the same width; consequently, large plants are expensive. However, it may be that you have one already in your garden which you may need to move to another position. This may easily be done by cutting round the roots with a spade at a distance from the main stem where they become fine and fibrous. The plant may then be moved to its new position with its ball of soil intact. Planting or transplanting may be done at any time in open weather between the end of September and the middle of April.

Buying Plants If the plants are to be bought, the choice of size will be governed by cost. Anything from 15 in. to 3 ft is suitable (smaller if you are prepared to wait and look after the plant, larger if you wish to fill up a hole in a shrub border by making another in your pocket). Some rhododendrons are grafted (on a *ponticum* stock) and some are layered (on their own roots). You will hear arguments in favour of each method, but there is no rigid rule. Some varieties are better one way and some the other. However, you should make sure which way the plant that you buy has been grown. If it has been grafted it will be necessary to watch for suckers as with a rose or a fruit-tree. (See Chapter Twelve.)

Treatment on Arrival   When the plant or plants arrive it may be necessary to soak them if they should be dry. Even if they do not appear to be dry it is an insurance to stand them in water until they stop bubbling. Any peat or leafmould used for planting should also be moist. The ball of soil should be left intact; no effort should be made to loosen the roots.

Taking out the Planting Hole   The soil should have been well prepared beforehand, as described in the last chapter, but the hole should not have been taken out. Now is the time to do this. It should be made in the prepared ground at least twice as big as the diameter of the ball of root of the rhododendron that is to be planted. Loosen up the soil at the bottom of the hole and refirm. Place in the rhododendron to a depth no deeper than it was planted

9. *Planting.* Left: *same level as before, soil beneath loosened.*
Right: *tread firmly. Note: peat or leafmould round the roots.*

before. Put peat round the roots, put the soil round the peat (by breaking down the sides of the hole rather than using the soil that has been removed) and tread up for the first time. To give good growth, a little cow manure may now be placed round the soil, away from the roots, but not too deep. The soil removed to make the hole should now be shovelled in and firmed.

Mulching If the planting is done in the early autumn, no mulch should be applied until the spring because, contrary to popular opinion, a mulch does not protect the plant from frost but insulates it from the stored heat in the soil. The roots are best protected from frost by firm treading.

Rhododendrons on a Lime Soil The foregoing method of planting applies to all rhododendrons on acid soil.

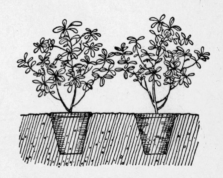

10. *In alkaline soils, small plants can be grown in pots plunged in the ground.*

Where it is desired to grow them on a limy soil it is necessary to prepare a bed of acid soil above the normal level. This ensures that lime does not seep through into the imported mixture. With the smaller plants, dwarf rhododendrons and azaleas, it may be possible to prepare pockets of peat, particularly on rock gardens, even where the natural soil is generally unsuitable, although it will probably be safer to grow the plants in pots and plunge them in the ground.

Pot Culture   Rhododendrons and azaleas are well suited to pot culture. The mixture should be one-third peat, one-third lime-free loam, one-third sand, with a 4-in. potful of hoof and horn meal to each barrowload of soil. Plenty of drainage in the way of crocks should cover the holes in the pots or tubs, and this should again be covered with coarse leafmould or peat. The method of potting is to place some soil over the peat, firm it, place in the plant and work in more soil round the roots, firming as you go, using a narrow piece of wood (or old label) as a rammer. The pot should not be filled too full with soil, in order to allow room for watering. Repotting rhododendrons and azaleas, particularly the dwarf evergreen greenhouse azaleas, is an exception to the rule that the ball of soil should not be disturbed: with these plants the outer soil should be removed by knocking the ball of soil against the potting bench. With the greenhouse rhododendrons, it is very important that the pots or tubs should not be too large.

CHAPTER TWELVE

FEEDING, AFTER-CARE AND CULTURE

FEEDING

PEAT and leafmould are the natural food of the rhododendron. It is remarkable how it seems to collect leaves
without any more help than the wind. You will often find
them underneath rhododendron bushes, from trees that
are quite some distance away.

Mulching   The best way to supplement this natural food
is by mulching with a mixture of peat or leafmould and
well-rotted cow manure. This should be prepared a year
beforehand, with a layer of cow manure sandwiched between layers of peat or leafmould in several tiers. When
this has rotted down to a succulent mixture, it should be

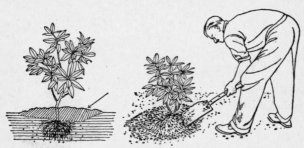

11. *Applying a mulch.* Left: *the plants will root up into the
peat mixture applied as shown on the right. The mulch
should be damped first, and the ground should be damped if
it is dry.*

79

spread round the roots of rhododendrons and azaleas in the spring—March to mid-April. Furthermore, it should be done only when the soil and the roots of the plant are well soaked with rain. The disadvantages of a mulch are that it will insulate the plant from stored heat in frosty weather (as mentioned in the last chapter) and that it will also provide a home for the vine weevil (*see* Chapter Thirteen, 'Pests and Diseases').

Other Feeds   There are many other ways of feeding rhododendrons. Guano is particularly good on light acid soils. Soot and dried blood give a nitrogenous manure in a mild form that will help to give good growth and colour to the foliage. Wood ash will provide a certain amount of potash which will encourage the production of flower bud.

Artificial Manures   It is often said that artificial manures are unsuitable for rhododendrons. This is not true, and great use is made of them in the United States—but, so far, little work or experiment has been done in this country. It is safe to say that poor growth may be stimulated by the application of sulphate of ammonia. It should be applied at the rate of about a small handful every three weeks from March to May. On the other hand, if the plant is growing well but failing to set flower bud for some reason other than a too-shady position, it may be encouraged to flower by giving it sulphate of potash on the same scale as the sulphate of ammonia for growth.

AFTER-CARE

Removing Dead Flowers   Just as an acid soil is essential before you start to grow a rhododendron or an azalea, the removal of the dead flowers is equally important if you are to go on from success to success. A rhododendron cannot produce a good crop of flower bud as well as a crop of seed. This, perhaps, is not quite so important with the azaleas, and the removal of the flower is certainly more difficult. The method is to remove the whole of the dead flower truss without breaking away any of the stem that will hold the flower buds that are to form the current

12. *Flower pick-ing; note clear break without damage to the branch or leaves.*

year's growth and next year's flower. The easiest way is to stand with your back to the sun (or to the light in a shady position) and to break the flower truss back-wards away from the light or sun. It will be found that it will snap off easily in this way; if it is bent towards the light it may just go on bending until it breaks off some of the stem. It is important to do this work early, so as not to damage the young growth. This is particularly difficult with azaleas, so it is fortunate that they are more able to stand the strain of bearing a crop of seed than rhododen-drons.

Removing Suckers The second most important work that has to be done to rhododendrons, and sometimes azaleas, is that of suckering. This is often neglected and often not thought of. Where a rhododendron has been grafted on to a *Rhododendron ponticum* stock or an azalea grafted on to *R. luteum* (*Azalea pontica*) it will be necessary to remove any suckers that come up from the

13. *Suckering— the spade must be the tool for this job, not the knife.*

base. For this reason I have said that it is advisable to find out how the plants have been propagated when you buy them from the nursery. The method of suckering is to chop down with a spade into the ground to remove the suckers below soil level. Do not cut off with a knife or sécateurs as this will only encourage the stock to make more growth. *R. ponticum* suckers may be distinguished by the fact that the leaves are darker and more pointed

generally than the hybrids that have been grafted on to
them. It is not so easy to distinguish the suckers of *R.
luteum* (*Azalea pontica*) and the leaves must be carefully
compared.

Pruning Rhododendrons and azaleas seldom need pruning, unless they become straggly or too big. If it should be

14. *Pruning.
Cut to an even
pattern. Inset
shows point at
which to make
the cut.*

required, the time to do this work is in March or April: it
can be left until after the flowers are over but this delays
the formation of new growth. When a rhododendron or
an azalea is pruned, the whole bush should be cut to an

83

even pattern. If odd branches are cut, here and there, they may not break into fresh growth and all the strength of the plant will go into those branches that remain; this will give a more uneven bush than before. Only bushes that are well established should be pruned. The place at which to make the cut is where a previous new growth has been made—this may be found by looking for a slight ring below which will be dormant growth buds. The pruned plants should not be fed until the new growth is well advanced.

Protection If you are trying to grow a rhododendron that may be a little tender for your district, it may be necessary to give it some protection during hard weather. This can be done by building a rough shelter round the plant with sticks and covering it with bracken or bamboo (if you happen to have a plantation).

CHAPTER THIRTEEN

PESTS AND DISEASES

Rhododendron Fly (also known as rhododendron bug and the lacewing fly) (*Leptobyrsa* (*Stephantis*) *rhododendri*, Horv.). The first sign of an attack by this pest will be that the leaves will become discoloured with many small yellow spots. These are due to punctures made by the insect when it lays its eggs. The eggs hatch out at the end of May and develop first of all into small bugs. Later on, these grow wings and become small flies. A bad attack can make a plant look very unhealthy, although it has seldom been known to be fatal. The fully grown insects lay their eggs on the young growth and the best method of destroying them is to spray early in their life season (end of May) while they are in the bug stage. The best material is a non-limy nicotine powder; if this is not available, DDT powder may be used or a wet spray containing nicotine and soft soap or DDT. The essential part of the operation is to spray the undersides of the leaves, as the insects live and lay their eggs there, seldom appearing on the top.

Vine Weevil (*Otiorrhynchus sulcatus*) This curious insect attacks other plants but it is particularly fond of the early-flowering rhododendrons. It eats the leaves in round circular patterns at the edge. These often appear to be machine-made. The fully grown insect is about ⅓ in. in length and dull black in colour. It appears in April and early May, feeding at night on the plant and hiding by day in stones, dead leaves and rubbish on the ground. Clean cultivation is a preventive measure, but this would preclude the use of a mulch. The simplest way to destroy this pest is probably to set traps consisting of pieces of sacking, cloth or corrugated paper at night, collecting them and burning them in the middle of the day (when the insects are hiding in them) and setting fresh traps in the evening.

Rhododendron Leaf Hopper (*Graphocephala coccinea*) This insect seems to cause little damage to rhododendrons. It appears in late June and looks like a small grasshopper. It can be seen and heard flicking about the bushes throughout the summer. It seems to feed on the buds and leaf-stems, making small punctures with its 'nose'. It may be destroyed by nicotine dust or by DDT. It does not appear to cause any definite damage although it has been suggested (but not yet definitely proved) that it helps the spread of the next trouble.

Bud Blast (or black bud or *Pycnostysanus* (*Sporocybe*) *azaleae*) This is a fungus which destroys the flower bud and, in severe cases, the growth bud. The effects are first seen as a discoloration, after which the bud goes quite black and minute hairs or spores may be seen on the surface. It has become more and more prevalent in the south of England during the last few years. No effective cure has yet been found and the safest plan is to pick off affected buds and to cut back affected growth, burning the dead buds and clippings. It is noticeable that this disease is less prevalent on heavier lime-free soil, and it may well be that some soil deficiency is a contributory factor. Feeding with sulphate of potash during April, May and June may increase a plant's resistance.

Bark Split This is not a disease, but rhododendrons with a high proportion of *griffithianum* or *arboreum* blood may suffer from splitting of the bark during very cold weather or when a severe frost comes early in the autumn or late in the spring. It is fatal only when the whole of the bark is cut away from the stem.

Failure to Set Flower Bud This is often due to a plant's growing too strongly or through lack of sunlight. Root pruning, by cutting round the roots with a spade and partially lifting the plant and refirming, will encourage a strong grower to flower. Removing overhanging branches to give more light or moving to a more open position may also be an effective cure. Feeding with sulphate of potash or any manure containing potash, but not containing lime or an alkaline substance, will also help to increase the amount of flower.

Burnt Foliage Certain rhododendrons, particularly those with *caucasicum* blood, may burn in the leaves until they are really well established. This seldom happens on plants that have been growing for some time and there is little need to worry. However, if a plant should be continually affected it would be advisable to move it to a more shady position.

Hanging Foliage Some rhododendrons, particularly Cynthia, hang their leaves during the winter. This is a natural habit of the plants, apparently to give protection to the stems. There is no need to worry about this, as the leaves will rise again in the spring.

Red Spider This is probably the only pest that affects azaleas and its presence is evidenced by a lack of vigour and health in the plant. The leaves look rusty and dispirited. The red spider may be seen as a small red mite which can be shaken off the plants. The method of destruction is an old one—dusting with flowers of sulphur. Perhaps it is more accurate to say that this keeps the spider away from the azaleas, as it does not seem to be killed by this treatment, only discouraged to the point of no return. It is also possible to spray with a weak tar-oil solution during the winter when the azaleas are dormant or to spray with a solution of malathion.

CHAPTER FOURTEEN

PROPAGATION AND HYBRIDIZATION

Seed This method of propagation applies chiefly to the rhododendron and azalea species. The method is to sow the seed thinly in the spring in pans containing peat mixed with sand. This should be well moistened, as it is not practicable to water the seedlings when they first germinate. The pans should be covered with a pane of glass and shaded with newspaper or similar material. They should stand in a warm frame or greenhouse until the young seedlings are large enough to handle. These should then be pricked out into boxes and grown on until they are large enough to be planted out in nursery beds.

Cuttings The only rhododendrons and azaleas that may be propagated by this means, for practical purposes, are the dwarfs. Cuttings should be made of half-ripe wood with a heel, if possible, during the early summer and

15. *A prepared cutting.*

dibbled into a warm frame or a propagating frame inside the greenhouse. The rooting medium should be a mixture of peat and sand. They should be kept moist and well shaded. The use of a hormone rooting preparation is an advantage. When rooted they should be potted on and later planted out into nursery beds, as for seedlings. The larger-leaved rhododendrons are now grown from cuttings by nurseries, both in this country and in the United States. However, the equipment required is expensive and not justified unless commercial production is required.

Grafting Most of the large-leaved rhododendrons, particularly the hardy hybrids and some of the azaleas, are

16. *Grafting,
fitting the scion
to the stock.*

propagated by this method. The stock, *R. ponticum* for rhododendrons and *R. luteum* (*A. pontica*) for azaleas, must be obtained by growing on seedlings for two or three years until they are about pencil thickness. These should then be potted and kept for another year in the pots. Grafting is usually done by means of the 'saddle graft', that is to say a wedge is made on the stock and a similar piece is taken out of the scion. The two are fitted together and bound with string or raffia. No wax is required. These should be placed in a propagating case and kept carefully watered until callusing starts. They should then be given more air and, when the union is complete, they should be transferred to a warm frame. After this, they may be planted out in nursery rows and grown on. The usual time to graft is in January or February in a warm house, which should be kept at an even temperature of 15° C. (60° F.).

Layering It is best to use an old plant with a number of branches growing near to the ground for this method of

17. *Layering. It may not always be necessary to use two pegs, only with large boughs when none smaller are available.*

propagation. A branch should be pegged down so that the young growth may be brought to just below ground level. A small hole should be made in the ground and the young shoots pegged down to a depth of 3 or 4 in. It is important to use a strong peg to hold these in position, and it is an advantage to have a short stake to hold upright the growth that remains out of the ground. The time taken to form roots varies considerably with different varieties. There are one or two that will root in a year, but most take two years and some three. It is wise to leave the plants three years before severing them from the parent bush. It should be mentioned that *loderi* and Britannia, particularly, take three years to form a root; even then, layered plants of these varieties are not as satisfactory as those that have been grafted.

Hybridization   This is the method of raising a new rhododendron. The most important thing is to ensure that the flowers used have not been previously pollinated by the bees and that they will not be pollinated again after the work has been done. A young flower should be taken that is about to open. The petals and stamens should be removed, taking care that the pollen from the stamens does not touch the stigma. This should then be left for a day or so to develop fully. Pollen should then be taken from the other variety, that it is desired to use as a parent, and placed on the stigma. This may be done by taking the stamens from the flowers of the other variety and brushing the pollen direct, or it may be done by using a camel's-hair brush to collect the pollen to apply to the stigma. If it is desired to make absolutely certain that there shall be no mixing by the bees, a light bag may be placed over the embryo seedpods after the pollination has taken place. When the seed is ripe in the autumn it should be collected, dried and separated—then sown as described on page 89.